On Value, Color, Composition... and Creativity

Copyright reserved 2020
Magunta Venkata Subba Reddy (alias Magunta Dayakar)

My Books on Art

How To Start A Painting And How To Plan It ?
How To Finish A Painting ?
Painting Landscapes From Imagination
Learn Composition and Create Beautiful Paintings
Simplified Color Schemes for Art Students
Capturing Movement in Portrait Painting
Who Fails As An Artist...? ... One who loves his Paintings
Straight Talk On Painting and Painter's Problems
Abstract Realistic Painting Approach: Why it is the right approach for artists?
My Books on What is Painting and How to Learn it?
Character of the Creator: Do you have it in you?
My Paintings of Abstract Realism
How to Teach Sketching for Adults through 4 Simple Lessons

Contents

This book will be useful for those kind of creative minds 1
Last Words..107
About Magunta Dayakar...108

This book will be useful for those kind of creative minds ...

For a student who is always searching for new knowledge, whenever he gets some information, even if it is from a single line, he will get excited for his newly found knowledge. Even though it's a single line information, as a knowledge seeker he knows it's value. He knows how to use that single line as a door to open more doors. That is the way creative mind works.
So this book will be useful for those kind of creative minds, who are always searching for new doors to open ...
All of the sayings in this book are chosen from my previous books along with some new ones. I hope reading all important things in one place will make for an exciting few hours of reading for any art student.
And, this is my fourteenth book. Writing these many books on painting is evoking different feelings in me which I could not describe ....

Magunta Dayakar

What is art?
The ultimate outcome of an artist's understanding of life.

Very good question it is.
Someone asked me once ..." Why are you keeping your painting appealing at every stage? "
Very good question it is.
I told him, " When you are working, if you feel your painting is coming out beautifully you will get more inspiration. That inspiration will give you more ideas about how it should be developed further. In this process you will enjoy every moment of your work. To get that feeling I keep my painting appealing at every stage."

Paint thick in light areas
Every master artist says "Paint thick in light areas, paint thin in dark areas." ... to understand this we need creative thinking.
Why do they say that? What does it mean? Usually they won't elaborate on this topic. They won't give much clarity on this! Why? Students don't know.
But we all know what they said is important otherwise why they would talk about it ? Is there any secret here? Or did those masters think, what they said would be understandable to the student? Is this true? Okay. I told you "There are no secrets, only approaches." Yes. It's true. Again we will

analyse those words … ***Paint thick in light areas, paint thin in dark areas.***
Paint thick in light areas …' Why we have to paint thick in light areas? '… This is the question we have to ask ourselves. Why we have to ask ourselves? Because nobody is there to answer for us. This is the way I used to question myself. An artist needs this kind of attitude. This is one of the key attributes of a creator. Every artist is a creator.
Again, coming to the topic … Paint thick in light areas… Why we have to paint thick in light areas? We will find the answer but for that we have to learn an approach to find answers.
We know what is light area. Where light falls that would be the light area in any space whether it is outdoors or interiors. The space which won't get light that would be the dark area. This is a very common thing in our day to day life. This we are experiencing everyday. What I am talking about is actual space where we would be a part. That is three dimensional. That three dimension space is not an illusion. It's real.
But if we want to paint the same scene it won't be real. We are creating an illusion on our canvas which is a picture space. This picture space would be divided into light and dark areas.
Paint thick in light areas…
So, as per masters saying, we should do our brush strokes with thick paint, vice versa dark areas with thin paint.
Just sort out the phrase .. Thick and Thin.
Thick paint will attract our eye. Thin paint won't attract.
Here the key lies.
In our actual lives we will only see the light, we won't see the dark. This is the way our vision works. So when you

paint the light areas with thick paint, it will attract the viewer's eye, vice versa if you paint dark areas with thin paint it won't attract the eye. That way the light effect will be real. The same we experience in real life.

If we have to create the same experience to the viewer on our picture space, we have to follow paint applications, the way our eye will see. Then we will get the light effect in our paintings. That's why every master artist says, **" Paint thick in light areas, paint thin in dark areas."**

Ignorance

Don't think art and life are two different things. In fact, both are one. Whatever happens in life the same would happen in art. Because of your ignorance you don't know that.

This is the key to do a successful painting

Whenever we are at work, we should observe our painting as a whole. Seeing it as a whole will solve many problems. What is this whole? I will explain it ... For example, take a family. We all have families. Family means a group of people who are related with each other and living under one roof. If all the family members cooperate with each other, that family will overcome all the obstacles of life and will live happily. The same way, imagine, if they don't cooperate with each other, if they are disconnected with each other, what is going to happen? Will they be able to face the problems of life? Will they live happily? You know the

answer. They will be in misery because they failed to live as a family.
Same thing happens in painting also.
Every shape, every color is related with each other and at the same time connected to the whole picture. If you don't manage those relations, the painting will miss the balance, harmony and unity. So as an artist you have to check continuously where you have to establish connections. This is the key to do a successful painting.

Value Plan

I will start painting with value plan, from that value plan I try to see the shapes which will tell some story about their structure. Then I will start to develop those structures and make them interrelated. When they start to evolve in this way, I feel I will get more insight. This insight will guide me to evolve more to understand the abstract beauty of Nature.

Painting eyes is no different than...

Many beginners think painting eyes is difficult. They think, they need to take extra care to paint them. In reality, this is a wrong notion.
Painting eyes is no different than working any other part of the figure. Dark tone, mid tone, light tone approach will work, just like with other parts of the face.

Every art form has this rhythm

We know rhythm in music. When sound moves upward and downward in a flow and sometimes with planned abruptness then we say its rhythmic. It means it is moving in certain order. If we don't feel that flow or order in it, we think it's not rhythmic. We say it is boring.
It is the same in painting. The shapes, colors, brush strokes, all these are moving in a flow, in an order, that we call rhythm. Every painting will have rhythm like music. In fact, every art form has this rhythm in it, including writing. Capturing this rhythm is one of the key factors for a successful painting.

That is maintaining harmony in panting.

Harmony - This is a technical word for an art student, not only for an art student but also to the student of music. Color harmony, rhythm, repetition, gradation, like these there are many words that exist in the science of painting. Not only in painting, in other subjects also few technical words surely exist. It would be a must for the student to learn about those technical words, otherwise they won't be good at their skills. Painting is no exception to that. There are many technical words that exist in painting. Harmony is one of those.
I would like to explain it as simply as possible rather than in an academic way which is very difficult to understand. For example, there are ten people living in a house in different age groups and different characters. If they live without conflicts, disturbances under one roof, we say

...they are living in harmony. That means living peacefully, supporting each other. Supporting each other ... this is the key line.

Here are some questions ... Why are they living under one roof? How are they connected with each other? Are they blood relatives or are they friends? Or ... is there some other connection? There must be some connection which makes them live under one roof.

But, that connection whatever it may be, is not enough to make them live in harmony, something more is required for that. They have to understand each other, they should not try to dominate each other, they should limit themselves to their spaces, then these things will help them to avoid unnecessary differences and conflicts between them. That leads to peacefulness. Different people, different age groups, different characters living under one roof without any disturbances, as one family ... this is harmony.

Artist job is also like that. He paints different shapes, different colors on canvas. They should act like a harmonious family on canvas. Of course it is the artist's job to make them like that on canvas. For that what he has to do? He has to distribute the shapes of different sizes, structures, and their colors depending upon their importance. What is this importance? That importance is what you want to tell to the viewer through your work. Every color, every shape will express something about themselves. So you must know how use a color or a shape to communicate your subject without disturbing other colors and shapes. That is maintaining harmony in panting.

An artist needs that skill

Emotional expression of an artist? ... What does it mean? Is he doing drawing or painting in some kind of emotional state? Is it true? Or false?

The one who is swayed by excitement, ecstasy, elation, for him, how is it possible to think coolly!

Without that state of mind how will he see his subject as a whole? Seeing the thing as a whole ... an artist needs that skill. Not only an artist, each and every one whether they are businessmen, scientists, actors, musicians, or anyone, who wants to think creatively they need that skill ... Seeing it as a whole. The whole means ... Inner self and Outer self.

Textures are that much powerful.

Textures. They will play a key role when you are structuring a painting because in this world everything has a texture. We are able to differentiate objects through their textures. For example look at the skin of a small baby and a ninety years old person. The skin of the baby is soft and tender whereas the old person's skin is rough and wrinkled. We know this because it's a part of our lives.

Just imagine ... if you paint rough and wrinkled skin for a baby, Will it not be like a scene from a horror movie. The same way if you paint soft and tender skin for an old person, won't it be like a scene from a fantasy movie? Sure. No doubt about it. Horror and fantasy film makers would do these kind tricks to achieve something unusual and odd just by changing textures.

Textures are that much powerful. Simply they will kill or

make alive our paintings. So we should understand their importance, they are not optional, they are a must.

They don't bother about creating a master piece

When your painting comes to an end, there won't be much work left to do and trying to work on it more is dangerous also. A little bit of unnecessary work will spoil the whole painting, it's like an unwanted guest in our house.
Through decades of experience what I understood is, for an artist finishing stage is very crucial. Amateurs will try to work more to finish a painting, they want to make it as a master piece but at the end they will lose it whereas experienced artists will spend considerable time just looking at it, to understand where they have to put their brush. In the end they will use minimum brush strokes to finish a painting. And also they don't bother about creating a master piece, all they do is they will work what is required to finish it. Remember this truth.

You are painting a composition rather than painting a subject

Once you choose the subject to paint, you have to use composition to work it. If you think consciously about it when you are in work, your work will lose its spontaneity. That means it will be rigid and artificial. Life will be missing in it.

To overcome this problem, go the other way. That is painting composition. You are painting a composition rather than painting a subject.
In this approach, the subject will be your starting point. Later it will be painting a composition, it will force you to think everything through composition point of view.

It's a mind game
Painting is fun if we know what we are doing and what we have to do. What I have realized while doing painting is, it's a mind game. It's easy to conquer the enemy who is outside rather than the one who is inside. Here the enemy is your urge to paint well. To satisfy that urge you should acquire the tools of the language of art. With the help of those tools along with your intuition you will be able to win the mind game.

What are the possibilities for you to make your painting successful?
With your intuition you are choosing a photo to paint. But you don't know whether your intuition is right or wrong? Anyway you have started it, because you are interested to paint. Doing painting will give you pleasure.
But, pleasure is different from reality. Your painting is a reality. If you don't paint it successfully, you will feel pain. Here the question is ... what are the possibilities for you to make your painting successful? Except if you are lucky

enough, possibility for your success is very less. Why is this? Because you have chosen the photo with your intuition. Without the support of convincing reasons your intuition won't work always. Luck won't favour us most of the times. So we need convincing reasons to make our intuition work in the right way. Understanding the science of painting will give you those convincing reasons.

Why do you have to change some of the colors?

Doing painting is not just copying what's in front of you, it may be Nature, a figure or a photo. Rather than copying it you have to make it into art. You need to add some things and exclude some things. It applies to colors also. Which color you have to keep which has to be replaced with another color. Why do you need to do this?

Why do you have to change some of the colors? What's the reason for that? ... That is, you need to do this to achieve color harmony.

Not only color harmony, it helps to achieve drama also in your work. Achieving drama is very essential to any art form whether it's painting, a novel or a movie.

Rules are only guide lines

In general, color theories say, when you use one predominant color along with its adjacent colors, you should use only its complementary but not its adjacent colors. In fact, it does not matter as long as you use the adjacent colors in a restricted manner. Because in all these schemes, all adjacent colors are having complementary color in them. So it won't be a problem if you use them in a restricted manner. Remember this ... rules are only guide lines. We can bend them without disturbing their essence.

To achieve visual beauty
Sometimes to achieve visual beauty we have to ignore some facts.

Edges
Never allow two object's edges to meet with each other, they will obstruct the viewer's eye movement from seeing the whole picture.

Perspective ... many art students are reluctant to learn it ... Why?
First we have to know clearly what is perspective. When we are seeing a scene in front of us, a tree in the foreground will appear in its original size, same tree in the middle ground will look smaller than its actual size, same tree which is in the distant ground will appear more smaller, sometimes almost insignificant. If we have to define it ... The object which appears larger when its nearer to us,

the same object looks smaller if the distance grows between it and us.

What does it mean? Change of appearance in its size. That means we are seeing different proportions of the same object size in changing distances. In reality the object size didn't change but to our eye it's appearing in different proportions with changing distances. That's why I said we can call it as ... proportion.

Many art students are reluctant to learn it ... Why? Because they feel it's a tedious subject and there is no fun and excitement. But it's not true. Once you learn the subject it will be fun to work with. The results will surprise you. Without perspective knowledge artist's paintings will appear weak and lacking strength. If a student wants true excitement from his work it's better to learn perspective.

I will tell you a quote from Leonardo da Vinci on perspective....There are three aspects to perspective. The first has to do with how the size of objects seems to diminish according to distance. The second, the manner in which colors change the farther away they are from the eye. The third defines how objects ought to be finished less carefully the farther away they are.

Paint the objects in less detail which are at a distance. What does that mean? Because you won't see the detail of the objects in the distance. So paint them in less detail. It's the way our eyes will see the things, same thing we have to do when we paint. Then only it looks natural. That is what Leonardo meant.

Overcoming those problems will make you a good artist

Just start your journey through painting, move along with it, you will begin to see new things, follow them with moment to moment interpretation. Then most of the times, things will be in your favour. Sometimes there may be problems also. Problems are part of the journey because you are travelling into new lands. When you are discovering new lands you are growing along with those experiences. All great people evolved that way.

In painting also it is the same. If you are doing mistakes mean you are exploring new lands. New territories will always bring new problems. Overcoming those problems will make you a good artist. I learned that way. Nobody was there to teach me. I explored everything on my own. So many failures, in between few successes. But I continued my journey, in that journey I started to learn from my failures. Learning from those failures made me what I am today. So take those failures as your teacher. When you become a teacher for yourself it would be a great gift from the skies. Enjoy it. Then you will start to enjoy your failures also.

The one who paints a picture must know this…

The king who has strength will enjoy ruling his kingdom. Of course he also has to know his boundaries. If he doesn't know his boundaries sometimes it may lead to him losing his kingdom also.

Like that doing painting is not just hard work, it's a game of creativity. The one who paints a picture must know when he should stop. Otherwise he will lose the painting like a king who oversteps his boundaries and loses the war.

Life tries to refine itself through art

I would like to tell you about a question one of my students asked me in class sometime ago. "Sir, you are talking about movement, it's not a thing to paint, then how to get it in painting "

Usually this is the question that haunts every art student. They struggle a lot to know the answer which is very difficult to get.

I told her, "When you are painting a landscape or some other scene what will you do? You will try to paint everything in that scene clearly, for example, sky, trees, water, figures and other things. Am I right? She nodded her head.

"But an object, whether it is a tree, a cloud, a ripple in the water, a man walking on the path... when they are in movement, are you able to see them clearly? "

" No sir..."

" There the key lies. What we are not able to see clearly that we are trying to paint with clarity in our work. It's against our way of seeing. So it causes loss of movement in our painting."

After a few moments she asked me, " I have understood what you said sir but ... how to paint it the way you are saying?

" It's a simple approach. When you are seeing a scene whether it is an outdoor scene one of indoors, usually your focus will be on one point, that we call focal point, other than that we won't see remaining scene clearly. It will be out of focus that means slightly blurred. Apply that principle when you paint. Paint focal point area with detail, reduce the detail in surrounding areas, remaining areas work suggestively. This approach will help you to achieve movement in your painting. Of course there are some more things which will enhance the movement but to begin this one will work. '

" Interesting " she said "It is similar to the way we act in life."

" Yes. Life tries to refine itself through art." I said.

This approach is must for any artist

When I was teaching painting for students, I used to tell them ... " Don't sit in front of your painting continuously, if you finish a shape or a part of it, get up from there and go back a few feet from the painting and observe what you have done. Check the values, is it lighter or darker than what's required ? and the color of the shape, is it connected or not to other shapes in the picture ?

This approach is must for any artist to get better results in his work. The problem with most of the beginners is they won't listen to this advice. They sit most of the time in front of the canvas, later they see things had gone wrong. By that time their work is already lost.

What is the reason for this?

Many artists who work from Photographs, they won't talk much about the photographs from which they worked. What is the reason for this? Do they feel working from photographs is inferior compared to working from life? Is this opinion true? Or is it a misconceived notion?

Textures are very important

Textures are very important to create an illusion of reality in paintings. Without textures we could not identify things. A green plastic ball and a green apple both are having more or less the same shape and color. How do we recognise one is a ball and other is an apple? Just because of their textures.

When we paint an apple we have to capture it's texture. If we don't ... what's going to happen? Our apple would look like a plastic ball. That means you are a failure. Textures are that much important, it will decide your success or failure.

There are two kinds of Textures. Tactile and Implied. Tactile is the actual texture which we will see in life. Implied texture is what we are creating in our work. The roughness of the tree trunk in nature is tactile texture and the smooth surface of an orange is also tactile textures. Some are rough

and some are soft. We feel them not only by sight but also with touch ...
When it comes to painting we only feel them by sight not by touch. We should create that illusion of textural feeling through Implied approach and also few things we have to know about them related to light.
Under a flash light we won't see the textures, same way in dark light also we won't see them. We will see true textures only in general light or soft light. When we paint textures we should understand the influences of light on them, otherwise they look artificial in our painting.

Most of the times it won't
This is what we have to be careful at every moment when we paint. We will start with one idea, after sometime we will move away from that unknowingly. It happens to many artists. Sometimes it will give good results, most of the times it won't.

Why artists paint mostly female nude?
For a long time I tried to find an answer for this question. I didn't get the answer. Through years of artistic growth, on one fine day, I got the answer.
The answer is ... Curves. Curves express beauty. All female forms are structured with curves. Male form does not have much of them. Observe...Everything in Nature is structured with Curves. We won't find those beautiful curves in manmade structures however skilfully they may

be structured.
That's why all great artists have been trying to experience Nature's divine beauty through painting the female form. This is the truth I have understood.

Composition Plan

When you plan to paint a picture, start with Composition Plan. Without composition plan your picture will be like a body without skeleton.

Balance ... Balance ... Balance ...

I am emphasizing on one thing ... Balance ... Balance ... Balance ...

Never forget this word. Always remember this. When you are working a painting just make that word ring in your mind unceasingly.

You should search for balance in your picture continuously, shape to shape, color to color, value to value, texture to texture ... it's an endless process till you finish your painting. A journey without rest. Relaxation comes only at the end when your work is finished.

Value Scale

If black is the extreme dark, white is the highest light. In between them you can see many variations of grey shades.

These grey shades are the effects of light. We call these variations as Value Scale. This value scale is the key to create depth in a painting.

Beauty lies ...
Beauty lies in every good art form. If the artists are not able to create the beauty in their work, then what is the point in becoming artists? Every artist has to understand the beauty. To understand it, they have to learn the basic principles of art.

Tints and Tones
Tints and tones will play a crucial role to create a successful painting. When you mix white with color it will become a tint. When you mix white with black it will become a grey. When you add a grey to color or a grey from its complementary color, it will become a tone. There are lighter tones, middle tones and darker tones. With these tones you can play with color temperature, color transition and many more things. It is a vast subject.

Biggest Secret
Every small or big things will play their role in our lives. To an artist, canvas is his life. So be alert. Try to know how the things will play out.

This is the biggest secret to become a successful painter.

Color Repetition

Color Repetition will help to achieve color balance. Eventually it leads to color harmony.

"How color harmony is achieved through repetition?" You may ask me.

My answer is ... suppose when you see yellow green in one place, automatically your eyes will try to find the same color in other places also. Once it finds the same color at a different point, again it will try to search in other places also till it is done seeing the whole painting. If you repeated the color properly it will achieve color balance and it results in ...color harmony. If you achieve balance and harmony, viewer will enjoy your painting.

That leads to failure of the painting

Every painting has light and dark areas. Plan which areas in your painting will be in the light, which areas will be in the dark. Usually light areas have warm colors and dark areas will be in cool colors. Use your color scheme with this understanding. In light areas don't put so many dark shapes, the same way don't place many strong light objects in dark areas. If you do that, it will disturb the light and dark balance. That leads to failure of the painting.

Equal Ratios
In your painting make either warm or cool color dominate depending upon your subject. Never use them in equal ratios.

The problem with portrait painting is ...
Are you an upcoming portrait painter? Or maybe you would like to become a portrait painter? Then you must know one thing.
The problem with portrait painting is getting the client to accept your work without any ifs and buts, without any arguments, without the need of any convincing words. Achieving this is a great success for any portrait artist. For this, not only do you need painting skills, more importantly you must understand the essence of portrait painting.

All great masters mastered this
Every color has a Value in grey scale. Practice a lot to see the color in it's value. This is the key to success to use your colors efficiently in your work. All great masters mastered this.

That is the worst moment in any artist's life

Doing a portrait is an adventurous journey? Is it true or is it an exaggeration?

Definitely it's not an exaggeration, it's true. It's a journey of uncertainty. However skilled the artist maybe, there will be a silent tension in him till the portrait is accepted by the client.

Why this silent tension? Is it happening with other kind of paintings like landscape, still life and human figure? If not, why is it only with portrait?

A simple reason lies here.

If you are a professional artist, when you paint any subject other than portrait, usually it would be good. People will like it at different levels depending upon their taste. For some people your work may be excellent, for some others it may be good or just okay. Here you won't lose anything. Because it's a general painting someone will buy it, if not now then later or in the worst case, you can hang it in your studio. So, there won't be any anxiety or tension for you if people won't like it.

But with portrait it's not like that. If the client is not satisfied with your work, he will reject it. Then what you will do with it? Nothing. Who will buy someone else's personal portrait? No one. Result ... You will lose time, you will lose money and more than that, you will lose confidence in your skills. Losing confidence is more dangerous than losing money. That is the worst moment in any artist's life.

To me every artist is a warrior

A person who has character never turns back, whatever happens. He is like a warrior. A true warrior never thinks

about death, he thinks only about how to conquer the enemy.
To me every artist is a warrior.
Warriors and artists are alike. Otherwise how do they become famous? How will they be admired? But to be a warrior how are they trained? They learn strategies of war, they practice and understand fighting skills. To become an artist we need to understand the character of a warrior.

Suppose rather than life, if you work from photographs ...

Key to success lies in your approach. When you are working from photos you don't need to limit yourself only to them. Start your journey from there. If you are painting a landscape, first study the things in the photo then study the same in the Nature. How they are appearing in photograph, how you are seeing them in nature ... analyse the differences.
In Nature you won't see much detail, you will see them as large masses whether it is trees, mountains, grounds etc... So avoid detail when you are working from photos. Paint everything as large masses. Don't see them as trees, grounds, mountains and skies, just treat them as small and large shapes. Study them as color masses. Observe the color, how it is changing from light to dark or warm to cool. Analyse color as a value. Reduce the number of values to a limited number. You should do this whether you work from a photograph or nature or life. Next, plan the composition ... which things you have to remove, add, refine ... this is interpretation.

You can apply this same approach to work portraits from photos. Instead of nature here you can study the faces from life. The face need not to be the face of person in the portrait. It can be any one's face, just like how you can study any tree in the nature, to understand basic structure of trees. That helps you to understand the structure of a face. With this understanding you will be able to bring life into your portrait along with features. I work this way. I feel comfortable in this approach. No one will bother whether you work from photos or life. At the end they will look at the portrait ... how good is it?

If you are an idealist ...

What you are practising is not a commercial commodity to make people pay money for your work. It's entertainment for the mind for people, which they are reluctant to pay for. They will pay for physical entertainment. Yours is not physical. Know this reality. Learning art, becoming an artist is enlightenment for your mind.
Why should they pay for your enlightenment? Think of it. This world is not that much idealistic. If you are an idealist, then that will be your problem.

That's why you need a plan

After working for long years, I have understood inspiration alone is not enough to start a painting. If you start with just inspiration somewhere in the middle of the painting you will become stuck with confusion, sometimes with frustration, not knowing what to do next. This one will happen to many students, amateur artists and occasionally to overconfident professionals also.

That's why you need a plan. You need to understand which value is in the figure in the photograph and which value corresponds to the background. It's better to start this way. They are positive and negative spaces. You need to achieve a relation between them. This is related to balance, harmony and unity.

It's not true

Most of the art students struggle a lot to choose a subject to paint. Usually they think that if the
subject is good, their painting will be beautiful. It's not true. If the subject is good, if their painting skills also will match with it, then definitely results will be good. But if their painting skills are not good enough, however good the subject is, it won't save their work. Results will be disastrous.

If you don't understand it, simply it will kill the portrait

When I was learning, I had done so many portraits because they gave me money for my survival. In those days I was living in a town, there you wouldn't find many buyers who would hang paintings in their houses. But I found few people who were willing to pay some money for their and their family member's portraits. When I was doing their portraits, mainly I faced problems with background. Backgrounds used to clash with the face. I suffered a lot to overcome that background problem. It took me a lot of time to understand where the problem was. I finally understood that it is the value relation between figure and background which is creating the problem. Once I realised that, it didn't take much time to overcome that problem. Why I am telling about this is, I would like to make you aware of the importance of value relation between figure and background in portrait painting. If you don't understand it, simply it will kill the portrait, however successfully you may work the face.

Hard edges will play key role

Purpose of the hard edge is to stop the eye movement. When a viewer's eye stops at hard edge he will feel the structural detail of the object. To make our learning simple, we call this structural detail as ... Form.
If viewer won't feel the form, he feels something wrong about what he is seeing. So hard edges will play key role in creating the feeling of form. But at the same time if you paint too many hard edges it also creates some odd feeling in him. That odd feeling would stop him from seeing the picture as a whole. Result ... movement stops.

Static means lifeless

Every Painting starts with an Idea. That Idea is your subject. That subject should not be static. Static means lifeless.

Nobody likes dead things.

If you are not good ...
People have a notion that, being a fine art artist, you have to sell your paintings, if you don't sell you are a failure. What a wrong notion! Selling paintings is not the only way to survive as a fine art artist. You could teach and paint for pleasure and ... you can write books on it if you are truly that good. If you are not good, if you are mediocre, you will face survival crisis. Not only in art, mediocrity faces crisis in every field, when economy is not positive.

If we paint Ears with clarity
Important part in the face is Ear. In fact, every part of the face is important. But ear is the part we generally ignore whenever we are looking at someone. Just recall your experiences of looking at others, did you pay attention to anyone's ears when you are talking with them? I don't think so, no one would bother about them. We concentrate only on facial expressions and bodily movements.
So, if we paint ears with clarity, viewer will feel something is off, with what he is seeing, because he won't see face that way in reality. Unknowingly it will disturb him, then he feels something is wrong with your painting. I don't need to say what will happen next. It's a failure.

Your whole has to dominate at the end

I have heard so many interesting notions from students about the eyes. Some students think working eyes is very difficult, that you have to put special attention. Some students feel, it's better to work the eyes at the end. Some others think you have to paint them with a lot of detail. Some hyper realist painters will work their each and every detail, showing the level of detail you would see only with a microscope. Different opinions. Different notions.

In my opinion you don't need to put any special attention to eyes. They are also part of the face like other parts. What we should realise is, when people are looking at you, they won't see all the shades of your eyes. Just they look at you and look at your eyes because your eyes are also looking at them. That's all.

If you work a lot of shades in the eyes the viewer may think that you have worked the eyes very well. But at the same time, he will ignore the painting as a whole. If the viewer says that you have painted eyes very well, that's a warning to you, don't take it as a compliment. He is appreciating a part of your work, not the whole. That means you have failed.

So, my suggestion is, don't put unnecessary attention on one area. Make sure, your whole has to dominate at the end, not a part of it.

Two Things

When an artist paints a picture, it has to achieve two things. (1) It should create an illusion for the Viewer, that he is a part of the scene. (2) At the same time he should feel what he is seeing has been painted by an artist.

Inspiration

Inspiration. We all know what it is and all of us experienced that feeling now and then. That inspiration will help us to try to do something best. Inspiration is the starting point to create anything, but there is so much journey between inspiration and creation.

For example, you have seen a beautiful girl, you are inspired by her beauty so you want to paint her. This is your emotional state. That emotion inspired you to create that beauty on your canvas. But I told you that there is so much journey between inspiration and creation.

Inspired by her beauty you want to paint her. This is start of your journey. Continuing the journey, facing the obstacles on the way, finally reaching destination ... so much is there. In your case your destination is creating her image with life on your canvas. For that you need planning, just like how you will make arrangements when you want to travel to faraway places.

Here your destination is painting the image of that beautiful lady. To do that you have to start with questions, like how you will question your travel agent about the travel plan. Instead of a travel plan, here it's the lady whom you want to paint ....Is she intelligent? Is she smart or cunning or soft and gentle? Which things interests her? Will she give value to human relations? Will she be helpful to others or is she selfish? How does she act in different situations? Like these you have to ask many questions, you have to try to find answers. If you find answers that too without being influenced, with detached and analytical mind then only you will know the truth about her. That means you have an understanding about her. After understanding it, you need to use technical skills to capture it on the canvas. Without technical skills you won't be able to capture it whatever understanding you may have on your subject. You need both. Without any one of them you will be a failure.

This is the law of reflection
Every color influences its surrounding colors. If we know this fact, it will help us to bring color harmony, unity and movement into paintings.

These kind of reflections takes place everywhere if we observe carefully. For example, observe a house or a tree or a person standing in outdoors, all these objects are affected by sky light and sky color. The same way sitting in interiors near colored light, that color of light will reflect on the person. Put two different colored plastic buckets near each other, you can see their reflection on each other. This is the law of reflection.

A good teacher
The one who has a commanding skills on subject, who has the best communication skills, who is able to understand student's absorbing levels and finally who is ready to share whatever he knows ...is a good teacher. This kind of teacher will help the students to attain the enlightenment of being an artist.

Don't try to paint everything

One important suggestion … whenever you paint drapery, don't create many folds. Limit them to two or three major folds followed by a few small folds. This approach will enhance the beauty of the picture along with movement.
I will tell you one incident which is good to recall...
When I was in the early days of learning painting, I painted a young lady's portrait who was wearing a Saree (Garment worn by Indian women). Usually Saree will have lots of folds which have varied edges. In my enthusiasm I tried to paint them all. Imagine, what happened in the end? It was a disaster. In those days I didn't understand the reason for the failure. It took me a few years to realise what mistake I had done. Once I realised, I never repeated that mistake.
That experience taught me, don't try to paint everything that you see in the picture. Just paint what you are seeing at first glance. Whatever you experience in that first glance, that should be the outcome of the painting.

Wrong Notion

There is a wrong notion in many of the art students and art lovers that realistic artists are able to paint only realistic paintings, abstract artists will be able to work only abstract paintings …similar notions are that oil painters are capable of working only in oils, water colourists only in water color and that acrylic painters are good at painting only in acrylics, the same way, Portrait painters do only portraits,

landscape artists work only landscapes, still life painters paint only still life…! This kind of opinion is false.
Art students once they are influenced by these kinds of notions, they will try to stick to one medium and one kind of subject. Then their artistic growth stops there. Art means creativity. Artist means creative person. Creative person should always continue the search for new paths. Picasso is one such example. He was a painter, sculptor, printmaker, ceramicist, stage designer, poet and playwright. He had started with realistic painting, then made the transition to cubism and from there experimented with many styles…. Creative instinct survives only in that way.

That creates movement

Figure and background space are moving in opposite directions to each other which creates a dynamic movement. Just recall this experience. You are sitting in a bus which is about to start. There is another bus also in the parking beside yours. After some time, you feel that bus has started to move. But within a few moments you realise, that it is the other bus which is moving rather than yours. Everyone would have this experience at some time or the other in daily life. We can apply that same principle to achieve movement in our painting. When the figure in portrait is looking in one direction, paint the background movement in opposite direction. This approach will create movement. Remember … When two things are moving in opposite directions.

Colorful

When you mix white with color it will become light. When it becomes light it will lose its color intensity. If you mix more white it will lose more of its intensity. If you mix black to darken the color, the same will happen. Becoming a tint or a shade, color will lose its vibrant nature. Then color in your painting will become chalky or muddy. .

To overcome that problem, instead of mixing color in light and dark, make it bright and dull. For that make your color as a tone. When your tone is on the lighter side it will be bright, when it is on darker side, that will be dull. Both tones will keep their color vibrancy. Then your painting will be colorful.

Your portrait will become special

Whenever we paint a portrait we will try to make it something extraordinary, a master piece. With this notion, we are doing a big blunder. Making something extraordinary, something special, the thought itself will put you in immense pressure. That pressure will push you to do unnecessary things. It leads to unsatisfactory results.

So, my suggestion is don't try to paint anything special. Do what is needed. It will become special. This the secret of great paintings.

When it comes to painting a portrait, just try to paint the subject the way he appears to you when you see him for the first time. No more no less. Your portrait will become special.

Those words truly shocked me

I will narrate you one experience of mine. This happened when I was learning painting. I had done a portrait of the Chairman of a town. I thought it came well. It had perfect features along with good blending of tones. I had taken the portrait to him to hand it over. In fact, I was very confident about my work. I didn't have any doubts about it.

When I went there, there were some other people also with him. They looked very curiously at my painting. Same was the case with the client.

For a few seconds no one spoke a single word. Simply there was silence. After some time, breaking that silence someone said, "It came well."

After hearing those words, I relaxed.

Then the chairman said, " … Dayakar, the portrait is really good. But … why did you paint that scar on my cheek? Why didn't you avoid it? Was it necessary to paint it?"

Believe me. Those words truly shocked me. I tried to digest his words. He has a knife scar on his cheek below the lower eye lid. I painted it as it is.

Those words taught me a lot. It was the moment which taught me that we should not paint whatever the photograph has. We have to add and remove few things to create the beauty in the painting. From that moment I changed. Without losing the features of the subject, I used to change the things whatever is required. A good experience. Those kinds of experiences would help us to grow to become successful. So, when someone comments your work don't get depressed. Learn from it. From this kind of learning you would become more certain about your work.

It is the case even for professional artists

Painting Children is a very difficult task for art students, in fact not just for art students, it is the case even for professional artists. Once the painting progresses the child's face starts to look like an adult.

Visual Mind

" ... Visual mind! What is it sir? " One of my students asked me.
" I don't like giving theoretical explanations, which will confuse you. I will explain it to you in simple words. For example, when you go to a decorative items shop to buy some object for your house, if you find something you like, automatically you are able to judge whether it will suit your interiors or not. In that moment you are able to see interior space of your house in your mind. That is visual mind. We all have it, but we use it in limited areas only. To be a successful painter we should apply it in your painting. For example, when you are making a brush stroke on the canvas you should know how it will connect with other strokes which you have already made. But the problem is when you are applying a brush stroke you won't able to see the remaining brush strokes on the canvas at that moment. But the visual mind can do that job for you. It's just like the way visual mind works when you are buying an object and judging whether it suits your interiors or not.
Think about it. When your visual mind can work in decor-

ative items shop why can't you make it work in your painting? You have to make it work. To be a successful artist you need this. I call this skill "Visual Imagination".

" … Visual Imagination? " she asked in a questioning manner.

" Yes. Visual Imagination. If you develop visual mind it will lead to visual imagination. To be a successful artist you should practice it."

Powerful Brush Strokes

When nature has temperature, why not in a painting, especially when art represents nature? Nature has four seasons. Every season has a specific temperature which will balance Nature to protect it from disasters. As long as Nature's temperature is in right balance our lives are also comfortable. If it loses balance what's going to happen? Our lives will be in danger. Painting is also like that.

When you are creating a part of Nature or life in your painting you have to create light in that part. How do you show that light? Light always has a certain temperature depending on the season and time of the day or night. When you create light in your painting you have to create that temperature also. If you don't create that temperature, the light in your painting won't look realistic. It results in … failure of painting.

One of my students asked me, " Sir, your brush strokes are very powerful. How did you get them? Is there any secret to achieving that level of skill?

I said to her …" I never think about brush strokes. And moreover such a thing does not exist."

" I don't understand what you are saying? What I know is your brush strokes are very powerful, that's why I want to learn them" She said, with a lot of confusion on her face.
I didn't answer her immediately. Not only her, so many art lovers praised my brush strokes. They used to say my brush strokes are very powerful. Most of my students also wanted to learn those brush strokes.
But always I tried to tell them that they have the wrong notion. In fact, brush strokes cannot be learned or practised. They will evolve through years of work along with understanding of language of art. The artists who have achieved in depth knowledge of the language of art, never think about brush strokes. Such a thought won't come into his mind, when he is working on a painting. All he thinks about are Value, Color, their relations and Compositional problems, along with trying to get unity in them. He has to to do that by applying paint on canvas with brush or knife. It is his act of painting.
Brush or knife or both are only his tools to apply paint on canvas. Results ... We are seeing the output of his soul search on the canvas via his brush and paint. People call it ... brush strokes, magical brush strokes, powerful brush strokes. All are false notions.
Brushes, Knives, Canvas and Paints are only artist's tools to communicate his flow of ideas. Other than that they have no importance. Those brushes, knives, paints and canvases are available to anyone who wants to buy. So my honest advice is don't try to learn brush strokes. You will never get them because they don't exist. Try to understand the process which resulted in those brush strokes. If you understand this, you are also able to produce those powerful brush strokes.

You should not overdo it
Every art form has a magic. You call it ... drama. It means exaggerating the elements but at the same time you should not overdo it. If you overdo it, viewers feel it's artificial. People won't like anything artificial. This is the reason for failure of so many artists' work.

Value and Temperature.
Artists paint in different approaches. Some artists use premix colors, some others paint directly from tube colors on pallet. I prefer premix colors. Premixing colors will help you to avoid many problems of value and temperature.

This is what artists have to achieve in their work
Realistic? Who cares? People are seeing it every moment from morning to night. Then where is the impact, when they see the same things on the artist's canvas? Why they have to respond to it? What they need is some magic or drama, whatever name you call it.

You may ask me then why people are praising with surprise when they see some paintings which look like a photograph?

Sure. But observe those people ... they are praising them

for the artist's craft rather than his creative skills. Best skills of craft will generate surprise but the response ends there. If you work with creative skills that will lead to magic. That magic will not only surprise the viewer but will also make them joyful. The feeling of surprise intertwined with joy will stay in their hearts for a long time. This is what artists have to achieve in their work. I call this experience ... magic.

All things depend upon surroundings
When it comes to physical things, there are no ordinary and extraordinary things existing in this world. Everything shines or loses by its surrounding atmosphere. Because of this fact, nineteenth century French romantic painter Eugène Delacroix said "Give me some *mud*, I *will make* of it the *skin* of Venus if you leave to me the choice of the *surroundings*." Here he emphasized the words ...' Surroundings.' Because of these surroundings ordinary things become beautiful, beautiful things turn ordinary.. When you paint a picture, if you want to create magic in that picture surroundings are more important. They are one of the key elements to create magic in painting.

It is one of the key elements in painting
When painting itself is a drama, there must be a hero. Without a hero drama won't survive. Value is the hero of that play.
It is one of the key elements in painting. It's the gradation

between highest light and extreme dark. Call them Greys. The interesting thing is all these greys are very important when you are using color. Reason ... Every color has a specific value in grey scale. For an example yellow is the lightest, and violet is the darkest value in grey scale.

Paintings based on truthful imagination

Becoming a great artist does not necessarily mean great technical skills. Reasonable understanding about the basic principles of art is sufficient. All you need is truthful imagination. What is this Truthful Imagination?
Imagination inspired by reality, follows reality and captures reality. you call it truthful imagination. When imagination goes beyond reality you call it fantasy.
Paintings based on truthful imagination whether they sell or not, they will be great paintings.

It's the nature of light

When your painting has the highest light it must be balanced with the highest dark. It's the nature of light. If you want to capture light in your painting you have to follow it. If you use yellow for your light area, it should be balanced with violet. For this purpose you have to choose a violet which has a dark value.

Different proportions

Background has certain value in value scale. All you have to do is paint that value by using color scheme which you have chosen. To do that you have to understand ... colors, values and their combinations in different proportions.

Medium is only a tool to paint your subject

Many art students think more about medium than subject. They think practising medium is learning about how to paint! It's a wrong notion!

In fact, medium is not important, learning about subject is important. That will make you an artist. How? You may ask me. I will answer it. Just think of this ... You want to paint something on canvas. The subject may be a still life, human figure, landscape or portrait. To paint your subject on canvas you need to use a medium. Depending upon your interest and comfort you will use a medium, that will be oil, water, acrylics or something else. Here medium is a tool for you to paint the subject.

Note this ... Medium is not a subject. Both are different. Once you finish your subject on canvas that will become a painting. If it turns out good everybody will appreciate... if it is still life, they will say "How beautiful those fruits are! Artist has infused life into them!" For other subjects whether it's a landscape, figure, portrait, they also say the same. They won't bother about which medium you have used. After that, someone may ask you which medium you used.

I hope now you have understood, subject is more important than medium, medium is only a tool to work on your subject. The key is the subject. When you have to paint a subject you have to know about it. For example, if you want to paint a fruit, you have to know which fruit it is, what is it's color, what kind of texture it has, where it is placed, from where light is falling on it, what are it's surroundings, how they are influencing it…. many questions. All these questions are connected to the subject rather than medium. I hope now you have understood, medium is only a tool to paint your subject, other than that it is no less, no more.

Value is more important than color

As an artist, you have to see color as a value rather than as a color. This is the most important thing to do a successful painting. There is one saying, … 'Value is more important than color. If your value is right your color also will be right.' Before impressionists all paintings were dominated by 'Value'. Since impressionist's era color started to dominate value. Now again, Value started to establish it's heroic role along with color.

Preconceived notions

Every painting is a new experience. You don't know what will happen next. This is the nature of painting. Because of this nature, doing painting always excites you as long as you are seeing it without any preconceived notions.

We call the result of this measuring 'Value'.

Why you are using that word ... Value? We need to use some word to describe. It is the word in terminology of art. First we can find out general meaning of that word. If you want to buy something it has some price. We are calling it as the value of the object. When it comes to the character of a person, we are used to saying, he has some values in life. In both these things, value is working as a measuring scale, either to indicate the price of the object or to define a person's character. Through these two examples we can say Value means measuring scale. In art also we will use it as a measuring scale. We use this measuring scale to judge the strength of varied greys between black and white. When you mix white with black it will become grey. You can mix many varied greys between black and white. To know how much light or how much dark they are, we need to measure them. We call the result of this measuring 'Value'.

How many greys you need to use ?

How many greys we should use in painting? In general we use five to nine greys from light grey to dark grey. But it depends upon how much light you would like to show in your painting.

We see many varied lights in nature. If you are standing in the open space, if the sky is illuminated with bright sun, you will see the bright light everywhere. In the same place in winter you won't see bright light, all you can see is soft and flat light. The same way when
you are sitting in a room in the evening, if light comes only from a window then most of the room will be in the dark

and there would be very less light. So depending upon these light ratios you have to decide how many greys you need to use.

Finally one must dominate

Between value and color, only one can dominate in painting, not both. But contemporary artists try to harmonise both. But it won't be possible. You may manage them to a certain extent but not fully. Finally one must dominate. It's like when we say about someone that he is a very open person, what does it mean? He won't hide anything, that means there is no mystery about him, he is like an open book. Color is like that. It's warm and open whereas value is mysterious. You could not play them equally, you must choose one of them as your key element.

That's why color is relative

On the face of it, yellows, oranges, reds are warm. Blues, greens violets are cool. This is the text book theory. But when it comes to applications every color will change from warm to cool or cool to warm.

For example green and blue, both are cool colors. But beside blue, green will appear as a warm color.

The reason ... Blue is a Primary color and it's cool. Whereas green is the mixture of yellow and blue. So in green, warm color yellow is there. That's why even though green is a cool color as per theory, in its relation to blue it will become a warm color. That's why color is relative. Its effect will be judged by its surrounding colors.

Halftone

Halftone is the most important thing to paint any form. Form means structure of the object or a figure. Halftone is the local color or original body color of the object. In every subject from fruits to human figure you can see halftones, where light ends, where shadow starts ... there we can see the halftones. In halftone area you won't see much light or dark. So it's easy to judge the color and value of halftone. If you know what's the color and value of your halftone, it will be the starting point for your successful journey to be an artist. From halftone you can go to light areas with changing values, same way you can move into dark area changing values.

Using Edges

One of my student asked me ... If we want three dimension illusion on canvas we should use hard edges very economically and mostly we have to paint with soft and blurred edges ? Could you explain it with some example?
Sure. For example if you are painting a huge boulder in the foreground, you can paint few hard edges on it. The main purpose of the hard edges is to give clarity of form so that the viewer will be able to see it clearly. If the same thing is placed in the middle ground the viewer could not see it with the same clarity as he had seen it in the foreground. So there if you paint unnecessary hard edges the boulder will

be visible with same clarity like in the foreground. Then what's going to happen? Three dimensional illusion would be lost. Result is your landscape painting would appear artificial and amateurish. That is failure. Next, is distant ground and sky. Avoid hard edges totally there. There we won't see anything clearly. So paint those areas totally with soft and blurred edges. This approach of using edges will achieve three dimensional illusion in painting.

Limited Colors

All great artists used limited colors in their work. Using more colors means more chances for failure. Limited color pallet will give you more control on your work. Myself I use very limited colors in my work. I never use more than five or six colors in any of my paintings however colorful they may appear at the end.

Today's art

The basic purpose of all arts is ... to entertain, to relax the people who are stressed with day to day survival. If any art is not achieving this basic purpose, then how can we call it art?
Today's art ... is it achieving this purpose? Is it entertaining the people? If it is not entertaining, then is it not losing its purpose? If an artist is not able to entertain the people how will they be attracted to him? If they are not attracted, how will they get educated by his work? Or get awareness by his art?

At first glance
When we see anything in nature at first glance we only see the light part of that. Light will make us to see the things.

The essence of the color
Understand the essence of the color rather than studying so many theories about it. Slowly with time you can study all those things. No need to be in a hurry. Remember this ... Mainly there are warm and cool colors like black and white. Every color matches with a value in grey scale. If you understand these values of color, If you are able to use them practically, you will have journeyed more than halfway towards the goal of using successful color applications in your work.

Don't get confused
Mid Tone or Half Tone or Local Color all are the same. So don't get confused.

Preconceived Notions
I used to see everything as shapes on picture space or in painting. This is an important point. Whatever you paint on

canvas don't see them as an object you know. That kind of seeing will distract you from their atmospheric influence. Every object is influenced by their surroundings. A white object in blue light won't appear as white. It will be affected by Blue light. If you don't have this understanding you will paint white object as white. Call this as ... Preconceived Notions.

Most of the students in their beginning days of learning used to paint with these preconceived notions. These preconceived notions are dangerous. They will ruin your painting.

Every artist works this way

Once an artist starts painting, his next step will be how to finish it. Some colors what he laid on canvas, he would leave as it is till the end. He won't touch them again. This one act shows there won't be many stages in working painting, only two stages are there.

One ... Starting.

Next ... Finishing.

This is the truth. I will work this way. I feel, either knowingly or unknowingly every artist works this way.

How to paint skin?

How to paint skin? Many art students and artists face this problem whenever they have to work a human figure. They will try to use different color shades to achieve the desired effect. At the end the subject may be colorful rather than looking like skin. In fact painting skin is no more different than painting a fruit or bowl. To do that, students have to understand Hue, Value, Intensity and Temperature of Color and how they will be influenced by surrounding things and light. If an art student learns these, painting skin is no more different than painting a tree, or a fruit or any other thing.

True color means Local color
What is the difference between local color and the color, we see on the object? For a painter to know about this is very very important. This is one of the key thing which influences the end results of any panting.
We see a person, an object or anything in light. Without light we won't see them. So light is the key to see anything. That means everything is affected by light. That light has some color depending upon its nature. If we see an object in sun light it will be affected by light yellowish white. The same way if the object is affected by some artificial light like red, yellow or blue in interiors, naturally the object will have some color of them . In essence when object is affected by light it absorbs color of that light.
Because of this we are not seeing the objects in their true colors. But to paint an object we have to know first its true color, then we have to add color of light for

that. This is the way painters work their pictures.
True color means local color.

These are some of the painter's keys

I have observed that many artists have been working with intense passion. But however hard they may work it would be futile, if they don't understand the Color Temperature, Color Proportions and Color Relations. These are some of the painter's keys to do a successful painting.

Viewer's Eye

The viewer's eye will move all over the picture space to enjoy the painting. Through arrangement of shapes and colors artist has to arrange the viewer's visual journey on the canvas. This journey will move along flow lines. These flow lines will create the movement in painting.

In fact painting nose is not difficult

When you paint nostrils, observe its structure, how its built. Many art students face the problem here. The edge of the nose which is triangular shaped is a little bit difficult for the student to understand. In fact painting nose is not difficult. Usually what would happen is, without understanding the structure student will try to paint it. It leads to unsatisfactory results.

Color Balance

Color Balance. It's one of the key things to do a successful painting and it's also a part of the composition.

Study the structure of lips
Usually students paint lips with more or less clear edges like nostrils. So they appear prominently in the face. This leads to disappointing results.
Lips are part of the face, so they won't have any clear edges. If you paint lips with clear edges they look artificial. Study the structure of lips, how their edges merge with surrounding skin. Observe, where they are merging where they are not.

Spatial Depth
From foreground to horizon what we see is space. We feel the depth in that space. The objects or figure which are in the foreground appear large, same things in the middle ground look smaller compared with foreground, the same things at horizon will seem very small to us. This you call spatial depth. This is the way we will see the world every day.
In creating painting also we have to do the same.

There the difficulty lies
Learning art is more difficult than any other subject. Being a writer I studied varied subjects from Physics to Philo-

sophy, Classics to Genetics. I understood understanding art is more difficult than any other subject. Reason...All subjects are concerned with a part of the universe but art ... it is concerned with the whole universe rather than a part of it....

This difficulty can be overcome with a lot of practice along with understanding elements of art and principles of composition. It will take few years to achieve certain level of command but it can be achieved if you are determined and if you are walking on the right path ...

Why do plein air paintings have some color freshness even if they are painted by amateurs? Usually color will lose its freshness by over mixing with other colors. In studio, you have plenty of time to mix colors so if you over do a little bit of it, it causes muddiness. That means losing freshness of color. In plein air it won't happen. The reason ... you won't have much time to work in outdoors like in studio. And for every hour direction of light changes, sometimes fast moving winds, heat, dust, unexpected rains along with many unforeseen problems will push you to do the things quickly. So you have to come to a quick judgement about shapes and colors in nature. Then you don't have much time to make your colors muddy. Result ... your colors will appear more fresh on the canvas.

Darks will become more Darker

For a student working from photos is not a wise thing. In photos darks will become more darker. So you are not able to judge color of dark. Darks are transparent, you won't be able to see that transparent nature in photos. And other

problem with photos is, they are condensed images of the vast nature. When you see the images of nature in small size print, like 8x10 inches … just imagine, what is there for you to see! Nothing. Those small photo prints will deceive you about the true essence of nature.
So, note this... without understanding nature and its wholeness working from photos will be hopeless.

But story does not end here
If you are working from imagination, you don't need to bother about working conditions of outdoor nor do you need to worry about the quality of reference sources to work in the studio. Just it is you and your studio.
But story does not end here.
Whatever imagination skills you will achieve, to make them work on canvas, you must learn about the elements of art, principles of composition. You call them as Science of Painting. This subject involves Value, Color, Composition and a few more things. These things will help you to structure the painting. If you want to paint good ones you have to learn them. If you want to paint from imagination you must know them because you have to create everything through your mind's eye. Nothing is in front of you but you have to structure them with balance, harmony and unity. Knowing the elements of art and principles of composition will help you to turn your imagination into reality on your canvas.

You don't know what you are going to do next on canvas

All of my landscapes I do from my imagination rather than working in plein air or from photos or from outdoor sketches. When you are working from plein air or from other sources you will have a picture that you want to paint. With value, color and composition you will be able to finish a painting. In this approach, your technical skills along with your interpretation of nature will play the key role.

When you are painting from imagination your technical skills will play a key role along with your past visual experiences, through them you have to create a painting. It's a difficult approach to work but it's exciting. That excitement would come out of unpredictability because you don't have any reference to follow. You don't know what you are going to do next on canvas.

This kind of unpredictability will continue till you finish the painting.

This common sense has another name ... Intuition

However spontaneous an artist maybe, he still requires a plan to paint a picture or a portrait. Usually everyone plans to a certain extent based on their knowledge. But to plan in the right approach, you need good knowledge. If not, your plan will go haywire. Not only in art, this disaster happens in any field if one is not equipped with sound knowledge along with common sense. This common sense has another name ... Intuition. This intuition comes to you from your life time experiences of pain, misery, humiliation, joy and happiness. Along with technical skills everyone needs this intuition, especially artists.

Here the portrait painter faces the problem

Portrait painting is tougher than any other subjects, whether it is landscape or Human figure or Still Life. Some say landscape painting is more difficult than portrait. Is it true? It is partially true. What is that partial truth?
When you paint a landscape, you have to achieve balance between many things. Sky, mountains, trees, foreground, middle ground, horizon, different colors and many more things ... all these things you have to relate to each other. That's why you require very good composition skills to paint a landscape. Whereas, to paint a portrait, there is only a face, drapery and background. Compared with landscape here the objects are much fewer. Achieving balance, harmony and unity between a few things is easier than achieving the same between more number of objects. I told you already, this opinion is only partially correct. The truth is different.
You may think compared with landscape painting, achieving unity between a few things in a portrait is easy. This opinion is also half-truth. When you don't have in depth understanding about portrait painting you will think like that. Some things you will know only through practical experience. Only when you accept a commission for a portrait, you will know the difference between doing a landscape and a portrait. In landscape painting you don't need to place

tints and tones exactly. You can move your brush freely little bit this way or that way. Nothing will go wrong. No one will complain. Sky, clouds, trees, foregrounds, middle ground or some other things won't complain about your carefree brush strokes as long as you balance them and unify them, but in portrait painting it's not like that. There won't be any freedom of brush strokes. Tints, tones and values should be applied strictly related to planes. A little bit of wrong placement will change the shape of the planes, that will change the features of the portrait. When features change, client will reject the painting. Because of changed features it would become someone else's portrait. Who will hang someone else's portrait in their house? And why should they pay for it? If you were a client, if you commissioned a portrait, will you pay for a portrait which is not having proper features? No one will pay.

Here the portrait painter faces the problem. He needs to capture the facial features exactly, at the same time he has to make his work an art piece. It should not look like a photograph, if it appears like a photograph it will lose it's painting value. Who will pay a big money for a photograph?

In summary, why portrait painting is difficult is, apart from maintaining the character of the painting, the artist has to capture exact features of the person as if he is alive on the canvas. For this he has to maintain tints, tones, values in their right places without any if's and but's. Wrong placement of two or three brush strokes will lead to failure. That means loss of money and confidence. I hope now you have understood why portrait painting is more difficult than other subjects.

It's not the end of the road

I work from photographs, I don't have much practice of working from life. I don't feel uneasy to say these words. Every artist says " If you want to be good at human figure, practice from life. Photographs are not sufficient to obtain sound knowledge." I also accept it. But in my situation, I didn't get the opportunity to practice from life. That's why I got used to painting from photographs.

I am very sure there are many people like me who haven't got proper opportunity to work from life. In fact, it doesn't matter. It's not the end of the road.

There are no fixed roads on your journey to become a successful artist. You can make that journey with whatever road is accessible to you. If there is no road then make one for yourself. This is the character of a creator. If you don't have this character whatever resources you may have, they won't take you anywhere. Just you will survive as a mediocre artist. Believe me.

Whether it is from life or photographs

As an artist, our every act is related to observation, analysis and interpretation. The question is ... how these things will work in our paintings? Once you know that, even without practising from life (except nude) you can paint everything as if working from life, sometimes even better than that.

It starts with observation and analysis follows. If you paint from a model or from Nature first you have to observe it. If it is a landscape, you have to see the sky, its clouds, its color and its light, then you will look at the mountains or distant space where horizon lies, how they are affected by sky light and atmosphere, then middle ground, foreground, trees and whatever else may be in the scene. You have to analyse how they are connected with each other with respect to shapes, value, color, edges and movement.

Once you have understood all of these then interpretation will start. That is the question of 'How to convey the essence of the scene on your canvas? ' This is the process, an artist requires to work on any subject whether it is from life or photographs.

This is the reason for failure for most of the portrait paintings

Sometime ago, after I finished a portrait, one of my students started examining it up close.

After a few minutes she said " Sir, this is surprising. When I was looking at the painting up close, I didn't see many colors or detail, it appeared like a very simple work. But ... when I stepped a few feet back, same painting looked stunning. I felt as if the person is sitting in front of me. Something magical."

Not only her, more or less everyone who sees my portraits used to say these words. What they said is true regarding color and detail. I used to avoid their prominence in my portraits. The reason ... we don't see color and detail whenever we see a person at first glance. We feel their presence, when we look at them, their color and details do not get our attention. Think about what I said for a moment, is it true or not? If it's true, why do we paint a lot of

detail and color in our work? Is it not against reality?
In general, many artists when they paint realistic portraits on their canvases they try to paint from finger tips to eye brows in detail. This kind of approach is contrary to our way of looking at people. This is the reason for failure for most of the portrait paintings. When you act against the laws of Nature it would become unnatural. It applies for portrait painting also.

Color represents Light
Color represents light. Light is the mother of all colors. So when your painting is dominated by color, it means you are creating light in it. Observe in nature, wherever you see more light there you won't feel any mystery or ambiguity. When there is no mystery there is no drama also. Light will give you warmness, joyfulness, happiness. So when you give importance to color rather than value your painting will be full of warmth and melody. But there won't be any mystery. When there is no mystery, there is no drama also.

Different combinations of shapes
What we paint on canvas is … life. If viewer has to feel that life on our canvas it needs to have the different combinations of shapes like in nature. Every art student should be conscious about this whenever he paints.

The same applies to artists

Most of the art students and upcoming artists will follow blindly successful artist's work. They will be influenced by their success but they won't try to understand the reasons for their success. Behind every success there is the artist's character. Not only artists, most of the people in different fields are influenced by success of others and blindly follow them without understanding their inner character which is behind their success. For example, If there is a beautiful girl, people will be attracted to her with desire. They won't try to understand her inside. That inside is her character. What we are seeing outside is a mask which she is wearing. Without understanding her character, if you just get influenced by her external beauty, what's going to happen in the end? You will be ruined. The same applies to artists who get influenced by other artist's work or their success, if they follow blindly.

When you are inspired by some beautiful work of another artist, you also want to paint something beautiful like him. So you will start to work. In the end you will lose it. You will become frustrated. You don't know the reason for your failure. That will lead to loss of self confidence.

Reason for this ...Just getting influenced by external beauty rather than searching for its inner truth which is the character of the other one's painting, which you can also call as originality. You failed to capture that character in your emotional state.

For example you are inspired by Renoir's colorful paintings. You wanted to copy one of his paintings so you did it. But you didn't get the melodious color feeling in his paintings. Instead of his melodious color, your colors are chalky, muddy and harsh. You are depressed with the outcome of your paintings. You don't know the reason, just you are confused. Before copying his work if you had tried to understand the reason for his successful color applications, you would not be frustrated. Renoir had understood color in depth but you did not. That is the cause for your failure. Inspiration is different from creation.

It creates visual beauty also

Coming to movement in painting...Just think, if you are unable to move your body, what will happen to you? How miserable your life will be? People think you are as good as dead. Why do they think that when you are still alive? Just you are not moving...so what? When there is no movement in you people think you are a dead person. Movement is life. Without it there is no life. In painting also it is the same. Painting is energy. Energy itself is a movement. No movement... No life. Your painting is no different from life. That is the importance of Movement. This movement gives not only life, it creates visual beauty also.

Those paintings have a story to tell...

Strong Light, Expression, Movement and Space will play the key role to structure a good painting.
we usually see babies and small children with laughing, smiling or crying expressions. It's not often we see them showing a curious or surprised expression. If they are in such moods, it means they are trying to learn something. These kind of gestures, moods or expressions, whatever

they may be, they are always an interesting experience to us. If an artist paints a picture with this kind of subject, whoever sees that painting, they will be moved by its inner strength. Because those paintings have a story to tell...

Lack of movement

Viewer must feel movement when he looks at a painting. If he doesn't feel it... it is a dead thing. Nobody wants to hang dead things on their walls. So, whatever subject you may work it must have Movement. If not... the painting becomes lifeless. A lifeless painting has no value.
The reason for many artist's failure in their work is... lack of movement.

Every painting has a focal point

Every painting has a focal point. What is focal point? ... Where the most interesting part of your subject lies in painting, that will be the focal point. At first glance our eyes will go there. After that the eye will roam all over the picture space, if the artist arranged everything intelligently. Where that focal point lies depends upon the subject and the artist's decision.
Focal Point is most important thing in the picture space. If it is placed wrongly, everything will go wrong in your painting. Never put your focal point in the centre of picture space, it should always be off centre.

Everything is connected to everything

A painting is becoming static, means it lacks movement. Every small thing will play a crucial role to keep that movement intact. Same way even the smallest thing can spoil it.

Remember this ... Everything is connected to everything. If you don't maintain that relation between shapes and spaces it will lead to loss of beauty in the painting.

Three value keys

There are three value keys to paint your picture. You can choose one of the keys depending upon your subject. (1) High Key (2) Low Key (3) Middle Key

High key means more light and less dark in the picture. In this key you should not use dark values more than 10 to 15 percent in your painting.

Low key means more darks and less light. Around 80 to 90 percent of the painting is in dark values. A small part is in high light values. Low key can be used in pictures to create ambiguity and mystery in painting. It is not useful for creating warm and pleasant feelings.

Middle key is almost flat without much contrast of light. It is useful when you want to paint a subject or a thing without any drama, it will also work for scenes which have flat light, such as scenes from rainy season, when there is no light in the sky.

You are used to seeing them as colors.
In black and white value scale you are painting in light and darks approach. So you will get depth in your picture. But when it comes color you don't know how to see them as light and darks. You are used to seeing them as colors.
To overcome this problem, you have to understand Value of color in black and white value scale.

Simplify your detail
Always remember this ... simplify your detail and show them at only where light falls. Then your painting will be more appealing.

Less is always better
Why did I choose a limited pallet? Less is always better. If you use only a few colors it's possible to achieve color harmony. In our lives also the same principle will work. For example, if you invite few guests to your birthday party, it's easy to look after their needs and make them comfortable. If it's the other way, if you invite many guests it's not possible to put your personal attention on them, that may lead to dissatisfaction in some people. Result ... Joyful mood of the party will be lost. Using more colors in your paintings is also the same.

Painting is a process of viewing
Painting is a process of viewing. So an artist must make that process comfortable for viewing. If not, the viewer will move his eyes away from the painting. That means failure of the artist's work.

Pleasant and exciting
Struggling with color theories won't help you much. Try to understand their essence, then your journey will be pleasant and exciting.

It should be always balanced
Once artist starts a painting, it should be always balanced, it should be always in harmony. Only then it looks appealing whenever you will see it. That appeal will inspire you to work with more intensity. To have this kind of intensity and inspiration you must maintain right balance of values and harmony till you finish the painting.

Technical skills combined with creative approach
Every artist has his own way of starting a painting. Even though starting is the same but every painting is a new experience. When it's a new experience it requires fresh

thinking otherwise problems won't be solved. This fresh thinking is a creative approach. Technical skills combined with creative approach will make our work alive.

As an artist you need both

To earn money for survival you need wealthy people but for inspiration you need ordinary people. If they respond to your work they will appreciate you tremendously. There won't be any limits. Just they put out everything they feel. As an artist you will be excited by their emotional expression. It will inspire you to work more. With wealthy people, usually it won't happen like that. Due to their habits most of them won't come out with their feelings in the open.

As an artist you need both ... inspiration and money. To achieve that you need to surprise the people of all sections in the society.

Harmony is very important

At every stage, at every moment I used to observe what I have done on picture space. It's a must. Because you are not copying or replicating or using some source to create a part of nature on your canvas. It's just your imagination, you are creating everything from imagination. Harmony is very important outcome of composition, it will come through proper relations of shapes, spaces, values, colours and many more things.

It will connect with every other thing in the painting
Whenever you start a painting it's the first thing you should plan, where you are going to place your focal point. Because it will connect with every other thing in the painting whether it's a shape or a color in your painting

In fact it will make the painting artificial
Many art students think, working in detail will make their painting natural and realistic. It's not true.. You should paint the way your eye will see it. It looks realistic.
Spend some time to study how your eye will see the things or nature or people or whatever the subject may be.

Feeling of light
Just putting dark values against light values won't give feeling of light.

This is the key to use Composition
When you are working, you have to use composition spontaneously. To use it spontaneously you should understand its essence rather than studying its structure. This is the key to use composition effectively.

Successful Painting

In fact practising art is developing our common sense. How we respond when we look at nature, the same feeling we have to create in our painting. That would be a successful painting.

Variety is one of the key

I would like to tell you one important thing which you should be aware of, when you are balancing one shape or mass with another one. The thumb rule is, never put an equal size of shape or mass to balance it. If you do that it will be symmetrical and boring. To avoid it, place a different size, that will avoid symmetrical shape and also give variety. Maintaining variety is one of the key things to a successful painting.

Color Contrast

Remember this ... color contrast should be used only where you want to catch viewer's attention.

That way we maintain Variety and Contrast

In life we always want some change. If we are living in cool places we would like to spend some time where the sun light is hot. It is vice versa for the people who live in hot countries.

The same in our painting also. If our painting is filled with hard and rough paint textures we need to make some areas soft and smooth. That way we maintain variety and contrast. To make a painting beautiful, variety and contrast are needed very much.

Eye Movement

Remember this… whenever you are creating horizontal shapes, connect them with curved shapes, which should be adjacent. Otherwise horizontal shapes stop the eye movement from going upward or downward.

Rather than their structures

Life and Nature, both are not static. So you have to paint their movement rather than their structures. Structures without movement will have no life. When you paint color as large masses it captures movement.

So much process involved
Generally we think, when people see our painting, simply they look at it, and if they like it they will see it for more time. It's true. But behind that looking, there's so much process involved.
That process has few things...
Eye entry, eye path, eye stoppings, focal point and roaming all over the painting.

Importance of Movement
Movement in painting...Just think, if you are unable to move your body, what will happen to you? How miserable your life will be? People think you are as good as dead. Why do they think that when you are still alive? Just you are not moving...so what? When there is no movement in you people think you are a dead person. Movement is life. Without it there is no life. In painting also it is the same. Painting is energy. Energy itself is a movement. No movement... No life. Your painting is no different from life. That is the importance of Movement. This movement gives not only life, it creates visual beauty also.

Where edge of the face meets the background
Look at the point where edge of the face meets the background. This is the most crucial area to achieve unity in painting. Here if your approach is not right, it will kill the unified effect in painting along with movement.

This is the essence of Color
We are doing a painting means we are creating light through colors. The purpose of color is to capture light. To capture light we can use all six colors which light has. If we don't use secondary color, it won't be a problem but if we miss any one of the primary colors in our work, it's like a crippled body which is not able to function fully. This is the essence of color.

Sharing his life time experience
You won't get all the knowledge from one or two books or a few books, however good they may be. Read as many books as possible. Every book will teach you something. You are reading a book means the artist cum author of that book is sharing his life time experience with you.

Colorful
Make your color as a tone. When your tone is on the lighter side it will be bright, when it is on darker side, that will be dull. Both tones will keep their color vibrancy. Then your painting will be colorful.

Colorful brush strokes

Working detail and painting colorful brush strokes will kill the spirit of the portrait. What you experience in the first glance that you should capture in your portrait. Client will feel thrilled when he looks at the picture. Reason … what you will experience in the first glance is the same thing he will experience on the canvas.

Make ordinary thing extraordinary

The essence of drama is …. To show it as extraordinary you have to show all surrounding things in less light. That means not in much focus. Then that ordinary thing is elevated. Then refine its structure more and more. In art, refinement will be done with Value, Color, Texture and many more. Then drama will come. When viewers see that ordinary thing in an extraordinary way, on your canvas they feel surprise. Then your painting will become successful. In every art form this works.

I am repeating these words …'In art... refinement will be done with Value, Color, Texture and many more.'

All you need is observation with thinking

One thing I understood long back, doing a successful painting is connected with your understanding of life and nature.

For example, how the sun appears in the evening, how the distant hills look like in that light, how much of the trees is visible, if there is water near us, how it appears, all these are related to our observation. To know these things you don't need to paint in outdoors. All you need is observation with thinking. Use that experience when you are doing painting.

It doesn't mean that you don't need to learn technical aspects of painting. Without any ifs and buts, I can say, you must learn about them but that knowledge alone is not enough, you also need to understand life and nature. Then, your understanding combined with technical knowledge will give the best results.

With right values
Balance should be achieved in painting first by arranging shapes with right values. After that think in terms of color. Here you require color scheme. Choosing right color scheme related to subject will help you to achieve the results what you expect.

Artist's work will become expressive
Every language has a grammar. Art also has its own grammar. That grammar is sketch, value, color and composition. By combining intuition and the language of art, artist's work will become expressive.

Color as large masses

Painting detail is different from making it appear as detail. If you try to paint detail it will appear unrealistic. If you paint things as large masses they will appear realistic because our eyes will see that way. That's why you have to use color as large masses.

Self discipline

Some people think creators don't need to bother about rules. That's a wrong notion. Every creative act needs self discipline. That you call understanding the rules.
Every subject has it's own rules. They will tell you what you should do what you should not do. But if you use any rules strictly without spontaneity, the work will lose it's beauty. Following any rule strictly will obstruct your growth. You should not follow rules blindly. Imitators will do that. Rules are only guidelines. Depending upon the situation you have to modify the rules. If you are following the rules strictly, it means you are not thinking. Without thinking there is no creativity

Habits die hard

Understanding color is so simple and yet so complex. Why? We are not used to seeing objects in a simple way. We make everything complex in life. So in understanding about color also we do the same thing. Habits die hard.

That is Creativity

An artist who is trained in language of art can work with any medium, whether its oil, acrylics, water color or any other, and he can work on any subject ...realistic, semi abstract or abstract painting. All he has to do is adapt to new paths. That is Creativity.

Artists doesn't need to stick to any one subject or any one medium for their lifetime as if it is their ancestor's property. If they try to work like that for whatever reasons, they won't enjoy the artisti

It starts with tinting

If you mix white with color it will become tint. That means pure color in the tube is lightened. Whenever we need to lighten the color. it starts with tinting.

Whenever you tint a color you must remember one thing ... you are tinting a color means you are reducing the color strength. So if you want to keep your color strength, use white with care. Remember the principle ... ' Less is always better. '

Tonal Value

Like color every tonal color also has some value. That value is measured through value scale or grey scale whatever name you may call it by. You call that value 'Tonal Value'. We paint most of the pictures in tonal colors so you should know the value of those colors in value scale. If you know this you will have a strong foundation to do a successful painting.

Tonal Color

If you mix achromatic grey into color to change it into a tone, it brings down the color strength. If you want to paint a colorful picture mix complementary grey into color. The resulting tone will have color strength. This you can also call … Tonal Color.

Space

Space can be used to create depth. Depth is three dimensional. To feel illusion of life on canvas, space has to be used with utmost care.

It's like tightrope walking

Painting a portrait means creating life. If not, it has no purpose. But when you are trying to capture movement in portrait, there is always a possibility of losing features of the concerned person to a certain extent. Then the client will reject your work. But at the same time, if you don't capture movement in portrait, it will become static. People will also not respond to it. It's like tightrope walking.

Placing the shapes in right places
We will see painting as a whole. It means the different shapes in the picture are connected to each other. If you place all the shapes in the right places, harmony will prevail in between them. Placing the shapes in right places can be achieved through balance. This balance can be achieved by not just placing the shapes in right places, you have to do the same with colors also.

Hue
Hue is the name of the color. Yellow, blue, red all are hues. Every color is a hue. Hue is only a technical term for color. Don't bother with it. Just ignore technical terms as much as possible. Understand their essence. You will be saved from confusion. Sometimes this confusion leads to frustration. I hope you understand my point. Next ... tint. If you mix white with color it will be a tint. What is tint? Just you are lightening the color by adding white. Next ... shade. Like tint if you mix black with color it will be a shade. It's darkening a color.

Search
If you get the habit of continuous search your artistic skills can grow without limit.

Artist creates life on canvas

God is a creator so creating something is his character. In that process he created Land, Water, Fire, Air and Sky. We call them as five elements of nature. Elements can be seen and also experienced physically. We are able to see land, water, fire and sky but we can only experience the sensation of air. For example when we are on the beach we experience it, our entire body will feel it's touch, our hair and clothes will move along with sweeping winds.

When god created humans he told them to use those five elements for their survival. Then a question started to arise in their mind, that was ... how to use them? They had understood quickly that they need some tools to use those elements. With time they invented few tools to use those elements for their survival. Their survival had begun that way. The same happened to artists also.

Every artist is a creator. When god creates life with elements, artist also creates life on his canvas. For that he also needs elements. His elements are Space, Form, Value, Color and Texture. These are his five elements. We call these ... Elements of Art.

To use these five elements artist also needs a few tools like the man in god's creation. So he started to invent tools to use the elements. They are ... Variety, Contrast, Repetition or Rhythm, Proportion, Balance and Focal Point. We call those tools as ... Principles of Composition. By using these principles of composition on elements of art, artist creates life on canvas like god.

He will think artist is not very skilled

In portrait painting whenever you paint hair it's better to avoid details. In life when we see a person, in the first glance we won't see his hair for much time. We will concentrate more on his face. We look at the hair as a mass rather than focus on it's details. So, if we work details of the hair it will appear artificial. When a part of the face appears artificial to the viewer, he will naturally think artist is not very skilled.

Where light falls

Always remember this ... simplify your detail and show them at only where light falls. Then your painting will be more appealing.

That obstructs movement

When you have to create movement in portrait, avoid working unnecessary detail. Wherever you work detail, eye will stay there. It results in loss of movement.
Value, color and edges will play a key role to achieve movement. I avoided painting strong values, colors and details in hair. If I paint details with strong values and colors, that will get viewer's attention, that obstructs movement.

What is Drawing?

Observation is the key to drawing. What is drawing? Drawing is nothing but using only a line and a curve. You should acquire the ability of using this line and curve to create different shapes and sizes. That means you have to understand the shapes and sizes of the things. This is seeing the things as an artist. We call it...learning to see. This is Observation.

Question yourself

In my opinion, lips and teeth are the most complicated parts of the face. You won't find clear edges there. They are intertwined with the adjacent skin parts. So, to work them needs a lot of observation.

Especially when your subject is laughing, if her teeth is flashing then your problems will be more.

Many students and artists face the problem here. They try to show the teeth and lips with clear form. Then it appears awkward and that will affect movement also. Laughing itself is a movement, you could not see a moving thing clearly so when you try to paint it with clarity … what's going to happen?

Think in the other way. Someone is laughing, will you able to see their lips and teeth clearly or just you are feeling their movement? Question yourself. You will get the answer. Paint the movement instead of teeth and lips.

Painting chin is difficult

For the beginner students painting chin is difficult. They try to paint chin clearly. In that process they will separate the chin from the neck. When the chin separated from the neck it appears artificial. Because chin and neck should not be separated. Chin is connected with neck. So paint them as if they are one shape. That will give you successful results.

Painting Hands

Usually painting hands will test your patience. But it's the same like painting face. Study the middle, light dark planes or values. It will solve the problem of painting hands.
But if you paint the hands in detail they will distract the viewer's eye from the face. If you think in your subject, hands are important regarding gesture then it's your judgment how much detail you need to paint.

Expression of the artist

Every piece of art piece is an expression of the artist. So there is no need to say art is personal. But if it is purely personal why are you showing it to the people? Why don't you keep it in between the four walls of your room? But you are not doing it. You are showing it to the people. You are expecting that they have to appreciate you. Is this not a contradiction? So no art is personal. Every art form should go to the people in the end. Purpose of art is to enlighten the people. That is it's ultimate purpose.

Entire painting will go wrong

However hard you work if you don't put your focal point in the right place, entire painting will go wrong.

The canvas comes alive with life
Every painting is a struggle however much experienced the artist may be. Success comes rarely, most of the times it is dissatisfaction. Don't call it failure … it is dissatisfaction. That's why whenever I start a painting, I won't think about how to finish it, I will just sail with it. New shapes will emerge, after sometime they may disappear, again some new shapes will emerge … this play will go on. In this process many images will appear, disappear on canvas, finally in one wonderful moment, the canvas comes alive with life.

It requires more than that
Many painters they work hard with total dedication, but they are not realizing working hard alone is not enough to capture the best on the canvas, it requires more than that. That is understanding the Language of Art.

Gives you the insight
Study of Composition will give you the insight to balance the things through harmony and unity. Then you will realise how art and life are intertwined.

Act of painting
The artist who has achieved in depth knowledge of the language of art never thinks about brush strokes. Such a thought won't come into artist's mind when he is working on a painting. All he thinks about are Value, Color, their relations and compositional problems along with trying to achieve unity in them. He has to do that by applying paint on canvas with brush or knife. It is his act of painting.

To create life
Artists paint not only to create life on canvas but also to feel life in themselves.

Artist's tools
Brushes, Knives, Canvas and Paints are only artist's tools to communicate his flow of ideas. Other than that, they have no importance. Those brushes, knives, canvases are available to anyone who wants to buy.

If the whole is right
Perfection! ... Nowhere it exists. Nature itself is not perfect. It is order in disorder. I always try to feel my painting

as whole. If the whole is right, the parts of the whole are also right.

Line

Line will be used to capture shapes, sizes and their proportions. Lines can be used as measuring scale. This measuring scale will decide the sizes of shapes and their proportions. Without the help of measuring scale of line, we can't capture three dimensional illusion of space on our two dimensional picture space.

Nature of the subject is like that

Every artist however skilled he maybe, always gets doubts on Composition, at least once in a while, if not every day. The nature of the subject is like that. If it is easy to understand, we won't be talking about it.

Creativity is the to key

Sketching will give Observation, Observation leads to Concentration, next Imagination will start. As a whole these three lead to Creativity. Creativity is the key to survival as an artist.

We must know our limits
We may have a lot of knowledge and skills, but if we try to use them all at once, we will be in confusion. Confusion leads to loss of self confidence, then you will enter into emptiness. That means beauty of life is lost. So what we should do is we must know our limits however knowledgeable we maybe. After all, we are humans. We have certain energy limits which should not be exhausted.

Simplicity
Many art students try to work their paintings with a lot of detail. Amateur writers will use so many words to narrate an incident. Both are ineffective. Then they get puzzled with why they didn't get the result they expected. The reason ... Lack of Simplicity. Not only in art, in life also we require Simplicity. To understand what simplicity is, one needs insight. This insight comes from understanding. Understanding comes from in depth study and analytical interpretation.

Abstract beauty of nature
I will start painting with Value Plan, from that value plan I try to see the shapes which will tell some story about their structure. Then I will start to develop their structures and make them interrelated. When they start to evolve that way, I feel I will get more insight. This insight will guide me to evolve more to understand the abstract beauty of nature.

Their true meaning.
'Creative brains, Creative approach, Something different, Totally unique ...' to everyone these are very familiar phrases but most of them are not able to understand their true meaning.

What is the reality?
Many people think what we are seeing is reality. Is it true? Scientifically it is not. Eyes will see everything upside down. The brain will map them to normal appearance. It is believed that for the first few days new borns see the world upside down, as their brain just hasn't learnt to flip the images yet.

Is it not amazing that what we are seeing with our eyes is not real? Then what is the reality?

That grand master is none other than ...
Whenever I start to paint my imaginary landscapes, I feel that I am playing chess with a grand master who has never been defeated. That grand master is none other than ... it's my Canvas.

Thin Line
There is a thin line between Reality and artistic interpretation of the Reality.

It's a wrong notion
Many laymen or mediocre artists think to teach art to a beginner is not a big issue. They think that someone who has some reasonable painting skills can teach to a beginner easily. This notion comes out of ignorance.
To paint for your sake you can manage with reasonable skills but to teach others a teacher requires good commanding skills. A teacher who is struggling to get his painting turn out well, how can he teach others?

Artificial and Amateurish
If you are painting a huge boulder in the foreground, you can paint few hard edges on it. The main purpose of the hard edges is to give clarity of form so that the viewer will be able to see it clearly. If the same thing is placed in the middle ground the viewer could not see it with the same clarity as he had seen it in the foreground. So there if you paint unnecessary hard edges the boulder will be visible with same clarity like in the foreground. Then what's going to happen? Three dimensional illusion would be lost. Result is your landscape painting would appear artificial and amateurish. That is failure

Mixing Color

Mixing color is only a part of the process of understanding color. While color is an ocean, mixing color is only a wave. Studying a wave is not enough to understand the mysteries of a sea. Studying wave means you are standing at the shore. From there you have to enter into the sea. From there, you have to travel to the deep dark mysteries of the ocean.

" I like red color because it expresses excitement, energy, passion, strength, aggressiveness and danger. " one painter says.

" I use yellow to express joy, happiness, idealism, imagination, hope, sunshine … " another painter comments.

" The artist used yellow, blue and red very powerfully. Lot of energy and vigour flowing in painting." one critic writes.

Are these statements true? I don't think so. The reason … color is relative. Its attribute depends on the surrounding colors. Once again we have to remember Delacroix words …" I can paint you the skin of Venus with mud , provided you let me surround it as I will."

Every color has a temperature

Every color has a temperature. Whenever the plane turns into another plane, color temperature plays a key role. As an artist if you don't understand this, your painting will never be a work of art.

Painted by right values
Whenever they see colourful paintings, many people think artist painted them with beautiful colors. In fact it is not true. They are painted with right values in proper harmony. You can work a beautiful painting with just yellow ochre, black with a little amount of red.

Like to Paint
I like to paint any subject with
1. Minimum brush strokes
2. Four or Five limited colors.
3. Five or Six values
4. Simplified Composition.

They are the outcome
Many artists say that Harmony and Unity are parts of the Composition whereas Movement belongs to elements. In fact, they are the outcome of using composition. They are neither elements nor principles. Just they are the outcome. I will explain you why. Elements are basics. You are not creating them. They already exist. Principles are the tools. You have to use them on elements like how diamonds are refined by experts. See... finally how the diamond shines in the expert's hands. That is the outcome. That shine is the outcome. It's neither an element nor principle. It's only out-

come. Movement, harmony and unity are also like that. Think with a little bit of sense.... for example you are eating food. Here food is an element. Eating is a principle. The taste what you feel when you are eating is an outcome. You may ask me.. ' Is painting itself not an outcome? ' Yes. You may get a painting. But where is the beauty? Without achieving unity, harmony and movement, how do you make your painting beautiful? If it's not beautiful what is it's worth, isn't it just like tasteless food? Who will eat tasteless food? A painting without beauty, how do you call it a painting? How do you call it an art piece? If it's not an art piece, how do you call yourself as an artist?

How he could stop it?

From poor to rich, ordinary person to celebrity, everyone needs confidence to survive in life. Most of the people will lose the confidence and strength when the problems surround them more and more. Whereas artists will become more hardened day by day, with time. Irrespective of miseries which they are facing, they will continue their work as if nothing exists in the world except their creative act. The reason ... whenever they are in work, they feel the energy. Energy is life. When a person is getting life from his work, how he could stop it, when life itself is invaluable?

Color Notions

For example when we see red color it will remind us of blood. Naturally it won't be pleasant. When we see yellow unknowingly, we will connect it with sunlight. When we see blue it will remind us of night. The same way when we see green, subconsciously we feel it's the color of nature. Depending upon our previous experiences we feel some notions about color

He doesn't know what it is!

Artists paint in outdoors, they work from models, objects, photos and imagination. They try to capture figures, objects and all of those with proper perfection as much as is humanly possible. Depending upon the artist skill levels they may succeed to a certain extent. Is it enough? Is there drama? Without drama where is the surprise? Without that element of surprise how can we call it Art? If they won't create drama in their paintings, they won't surprise the viewers. That means failure.

This is the problem many artists usually face. That's why whatever they work, however much they try, at the end they feel dissatisfaction, if not immediately it would be later. That's the reason ... even though an artist enjoys his work after he finishes, when he looked at it after sometime, he would start to feel doubt about the quality of his work. He will feel the painting lacks something, but he doesn't know what it is. This is a very common experience for most of the artists, whenever they see their past works.

Artistic Growth

Most of the people have a tendency, that whenever they see a painting, it does not matter who painted it they will praise it ..." It's good."
It is their good heartedness towards painters. But it is creating a big problem for artist's growth. Most of the artists believe what people are saying is true. What will happen then? They will lose their burning urge to learn. They try to stick to the same kind of work for which people are praising them. To most of the artists it will happen. Results ... They remain mediocre.

Influences

When you see the red color subconsciously you get thoughts of blood. The same happens with yellow, green, blue or any other color. This we call relative effect. Suppose someone who has never seen blood, if he has seen only red roses what goes through his mind, when he sees red? Just think about it. He will remember red roses. It happens with every color. The effect of the color is relative to our previous experiences. These will influence us whenever we see a color. Artists have to use these influences in their work depending upon their subject's requirements.
For example red and rose have different influences on us. If you use red in your painting it will evoke the feeling of blood, danger, extreme alertness, the same way if you use a rose it will evoke pleasant sensations related to rose flowers, rose toned female faces. These are the influences

of those colors on us. When we paint we should keep those effects in our mind.

Your path should be right

If you don't know what you have to learn, your efforts will be wasted in the name of learning. First put in an effort to know what you have to learn. Knowing what to learn is the first crucial step for any learner. Here many people go on the wrong path. Remember ... Your path should be right to reach the destination.

Second Skin

Someone asked me, do you paint every day or does it depend on certain factors?

My answer is ... sometimes I paint every day; Sometimes I don't. No particular hours. Just I do whenever I feel convenient. I don't believe in moods. When you have to work you should work. I believe in this kind of mood. Creative instinct should be a second skin for any artist.

However successful you are ...

Learn Drawing. It is like the spinal cord of art. All great masters including modern and abstract artists mastered this. If you don't have the drawing skills however successful you are as an artist, you won't have the pride to call yourself an Artist.

The same problem
To communicate your feelings to others you need strong technical skills. In other words...Literacy. A man who is not having education may have a very good imagination about nature's beauty. But to write about it he needs good command on language. But it's not possible for him because he is not educated; he doesn't have command of language skills.
Like that, artists also face the same problem.
To communicate to viewers what they feel, they require sound knowledge in visual language. But in the name of modern, abstract or other names of art they ignore the visual language. They stopped practising sketching, they do not possess in-depth knowledge of color and composition and they start to believe in the emotional state of mind. They think they will express their feelings strongly with emotional mind instead of using strong language skills! How is this possible?

Only if we achieve
Truthfully speaking, Painting is an act which enlightens our mind. But this enlightenment, relaxation and calmness would happen only if we achieve artistic growth, that means learning technical and creative skills. A good teacher will help students to achieve that.

Learning Painting

This is the problem most of the art students face when they are learning painting. After learning a little bit of sketching they start to copy from prints. They expect their painting should be more or less close to the printed copy of the painting. But those images are painted by professional artists. How is it possible for a level two student to paint like a level ten professional? It's like high school physics student trying to understand research level physics.

You should evolve slowly without any hurry. At the same time try to know what you want to achieve in the end, but your focus should be in the present. Then you will become good with time.

That is Character

' What is the Character of a Creator? '... many people are asking me this question.

What is character?

Sometimes we appreciate greatness of some people. We admire them. We try to follow them. We will make them as our heroes.

Why do we admire them like that?

Because they had some qualities, traits, which made them as heroes, legends and all time greats.

Character means having these qualities, traits. A person has character means he is selfless, ready to sacrifice to achieve his dreams, ready to lose anything to reach his destination. That is character.

Warriors and Artists

To become an artist we need to understand the character of a warrior. We should try to become like that. In history only Warriors and Artists will be remembered more than anyone. Perhaps the reason is, they are the creators and they are also the destroyers. By conquering other kingdoms warriors will create new states. To achieve this, they will destroy the existing states where as artists will lose themselves in the process of creation. That is the greatness of the artist. To create a new world on two dimensional canvas they are ready to destroy so many canvases. In this process so much suffering, pain and agony they have to experience. Great things never come to you cheaply. The entire world, irrespective of races, countries talk about Leonardo da Vinci's Monalisa.

Light and Darks

Value is related to light. Where there is light there is darkness as well. It's like day and night. We see the light in day time, we feel the darkness in nights. This is the light and dark of the nature. We artists try to create this light and darks of the nature in our paintings also. Capturing these light and darks, technically we call it ... Value.

We can ask ourselves
Character demands continuous learning, courage to sacrifice, and risk taking. We can ask ourselves sincerely ...' how many artists are having this character?

Mind's Eye
Whatever you want to show the viewer in your finished painting, you have to see the basic structure of it in your in your mind's eye. This is called Visual Imagination. When you are able to get this visual imagination, then your tools will follow. That is the coordination between mind, eye, hand and tools. Every Artist requires these visual imagination skills when it comes to applications on picture space or any actual space.

Temperature
Nature has sun light or moon light to make us feel that temperature. But we don't have those resources when we paint. Whatever we do we have to do it only with colors. Warm and cool colors will be useful for this purpose. In general warm colors represent light whereas cool colors will work for shadows. Depending upon the intensity of light you should use these warm and cool colors in required balance. Only then you will get proper light in your pairing. If not it would behave like nature which loses seasonal balance.

What is the language of art?

Many people are asking me ...' what is the language of art?' It's not possible for me to answer everyone individually. Here I am explaining about it.

'Every subject has its own language. For example, if you want to learn English, you should start with alphabets, words, sentences, grammar and like that. Once you study these things well, then you are able to structure a sentence to communicate whatever you want to say. Making sentences into a paragraph, from paragraphs to pages, to write you need a lot of practice and a lot of reading. After that writing making it readable is the next step. The one who makes his writing readable will become a popular writer, his writing would be called as popular writing. Example ... Popular Novels or Fiction.

Art also has its own language ... Line, Shape, Space, Form, Value, Color, Composition and many more are there in the language of art. If someone wants to become a professional artist, they must study these things at least to a certain extent. These same things apply in all visual art related fields.

The Value

Usually in the foreground the value would be stronger, in middle ground it would be less stronger, in distance it would be in lighter tones.

A war with ourselves

Nature is vast and mysterious and there are many ambiguities which we don't know. When we are trying to recreate Nature on our canvas in its essence it will be always a war with ourselves however knowledgeable we may be.

Beauty of Life

I am trying to find the beauty of life and where it lies. Beauty and problem lie side by side. If you remove the problem, then beauty only exists. Few human beings who try to live always creatively, sometimes suffer from emptiness. The reason... they want to do so much in
a very short time.
It's like trying to finish painting quickly or any creative work. When an artist tries to finish his painting as quickly as possible what's going to happen? The very first thing, he won't enjoy his work and next, his mind feels pressure which leads to loss of interest in his work. Results ... he will try to find some other ways to survive, that means change of profession. All of this happens due to trying to achieve things quickly. Then beauty of life is lost; depression or problem remains.

Continuous Learning

When you are explaining the soul of any subject to others you will enjoy it. You will be enlightened yourself. You are explaining to others means you are learning. That's why true artists and teachers don't keep any secrets with them, they will reveal everything they know. That's their way of learning. Continuous learning will make them masters.

They expect appreciation

Children paint without bothering about following any rules. They just feel joy when something comes out of the paper when they paint. That moment will make them joyful and later they will forget about what they painted and they won't even bother where they kept their work and moreover they also don't care much about others appreciation. To put it simply, they are not expecting any returns from their work. They do it for pure pleasure. But when it comes to adults or professional artists it's a different story. If it is adults who paint as a pastime, they expect appreciation, if they feel that they are at professional level then they expect money and appreciation. How can they paint like children when they expect other's recognition for their work? Unlike children, if they want returns for their work, they should learn language of art, they should follow all structural principles like an architect, if they don't follow, the structure will collapse.

Failure of Painting

Nature has four seasons. Every season has a specific temperature which will balance nature to protect it from disasters. As long as nature's temperature is in right balance our lives are also comfortable. If it loses balance what's going to happen? Our lives will be in danger. Painting is also like that.

When you are creating a part of nature or life in your painting you have to create light in that part. How do you show that light? Light always has a certain temperature depending on season and time of the day or night. When you create light in your painting you have to create that temperature also. If you don't create that temperature, the light in your painting won't look realistic. It results in … failure of painting.

It will lead to creativity.

Every learning starts with copying. For example, take a small child, she will learn everything from her surroundings, how to talk, how to walk, how to eat, how to behave ...everything. When she starts to grow, she will come out of her surroundings and step outside. There she will see, meet and interact with more people and will see more things. Whatever she is attracted to, she will try to absorb it like what she had done as an infant, as a baby. These are all copying. From this copying, she will learn more about life and world. From that stage she will enter onto the next stage. Then she starts to think about what she likes and what she dislikes through her experiences. This is the transition from stage of copying to individuality. Doctors, lawyers, economists, actors, musicians and with everybody this pattern will happen.

First, they work with somebody or some firm. They will learn what others are doing there. After years of experience they will start doing things on their own based on their experiences. This pattern will happen everywhere. So in this world everyone starts their learning from copying. Years of copying gives them confidence to do things on their own. Next, if you have a burning urge to do something different, then it will lead to creativity.

Your drawing look right

Angles will tell us how the object is situated in space. If you capture the angle of the object the drawing appears right, otherwise it looks unbalanced. If something is unbalanced our eye will sense something is not right with it. Your drawing is also no different. So when you draw, observe the angle of the object in your drawing. Proportions and angles will make your drawing look right for the eye.

Avoid unnecessary hard edges

There are three kind of edges, hard, soft and blurred edges. Let me tell you first when and where we have to use these edges. Suppose if you are painting a landscape, it's divided into foreground, middle ground, distant ground which is at the horizon and sky. Foreground is the closest space to us, there we have to work detail, here you can use few hard edges wherever you would like get viewer's attention, reduce the detail when you paint middle ground ....
Avoid unnecessary hard edges in the middle ground, paint most of it with soft and blurred edges. This way viewer's attention span will be reduced when he looks at the middle ground, next it's distant ground, there you avoid hard edges

totally, paint only with soft and blurred edges, the same applies to sky area also.

Human figure is also a shape
Many art students think, sketching human figure is difficult. In fact

it is not true. Human figure is also a shape like other things. Then where the problem lies? It's all related to our familiarity with the things. Because we are human beings, we are very familiar with its structure. That's why we will be able to identify even the smallest mistake in a drawing of a human being. That's the reason why we feel sketching and painting a human figure is difficult.
For example, if you paint a lion, except if you make major mistakes with its structure can anyone recognise mistakes in it? No way. Why? They would have never spent time with a lion with the level of closeness as they would have with another human being. That's why familiarity is the key here. Even in life also if we know someone very closely, we also know his flaws. In drawing also it's the same. That's why I don't find any difference between still life, landscape or human figure for drawing. All are shapes. Just shapes. One line and one curve are enough to draw any shape. Anyone can draw a line and curve. What greatness lies in drawing them? In fact, anyone can do basic sketching if you put them in the right direction. It's all about observation and a few techniques.

Detachedness

Once we achieve a great success what we feel first is elation, after some time it will turn into relaxation. We will enjoy the success of our hard work in these two stages. When we experienced them fully, our mind will enter into detachedness. Why this detachedness? It's like an adventurous journey. The one who is doing an adventurous journey feels elation and relaxation at every stage and at the end of his goal. But within no time he would come out of it by thinking about going to the next place. He will start to think about it. In that process of thinking about next day's journey he would become detached with the success which happened already. Suppose If he didn't have any more places to travel then there won't be detachedness at least for sometime, or at least till he gets bored with his inactive life.

It is inborn

Imaginary scale. You can use it instead of measuring scale. To use this one, you need the help of your mind. That's why you should learn how to use your mind, rather than depending on measuring aids.

In fact, it's not difficult to use. we use it every day in our lives. We use it to measure height, width, depth and distances through our visual eye or as I call it "mind's eye", whenever we see new objects and spaces to walk. For example, when we have to walk in a long corridor, unknowingly we will judge its length. The same way we used to measure everything, whether they are figures, objects, rivers etc.

This our natural instinct. It is inborn, we have it for our survival. The same skills we have to use in our drawing to measure the proportions of shapes and their relations through height and width. Once we start to use it, it will be a child's play for us.

Failures and Mistakes

Failures and mistakes, both are different. For example when you are doing a painting, if you didn't get the result you expected then with frustration if you stopped doing painting forever … it's a failure. Instead of that, if you will struggle to find the cause for your failure and try to correct it, it is not a failure. It will be correcting a mistake.
I will explain about this more.
For example … You tried to do painting well but you didn't get it. So you stopped to do painting forever because you thought you are not born for it and you didn't have the right talent to be an artist. With this kind of thinking if you stopped to do painting that would a failure because you said good bye to it forever. But if you will try to continue your struggle to find the problem which caused that failure, finally knowing it and overcame it … that is called correcting a mistake.
In fact, in doing painting there won't be any failures. It's all mistakes. Professional artist will try to correct as many mistakes as possible in his work whereas an amateur will try to ignore them and convince himself what he did is good. This attitude leads to failure.

Last Words

I have bought and read most of the books on painting. After reading hundreds of books in a few years time, then I understood how to read them in the right way.

About Magunta Dayakar

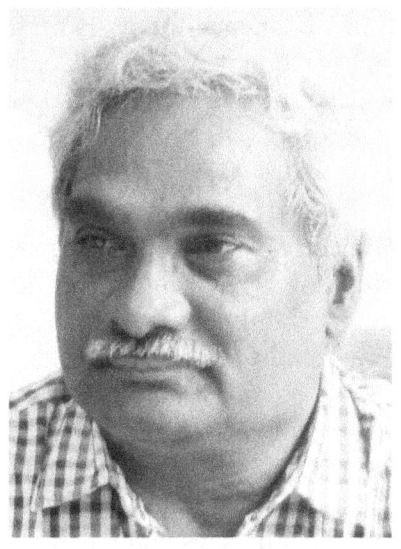

Magunta Dayakar was born in 1951 in Andhra Pradesh, India. After discontinuing his studies in graduation, he did different things in different periods. He had become a popular fiction writer in his native language Telugu, credited with thirty-five novels. He had worked as an editor and also published a feature magazine for a brief period. He scripted, acted and directed two feature films. He worked for Spectra and Coca Cola India as an artist. He ran Creative Painting School for children in Hyderabad for nearly 15 years.

He believes artist must be able to do all kind of subjects from Still life to Portraits, different styles like Abstract to Realistic Painting rather than limiting himself to one or two subjects and styles, he strongly feels that is the only way any artist will be alive in his journey to understand the Science of Painting.

Now, most of the time he is working on writing books on painting to bring awareness about the Science of Painting. He defines science of painting as …"Just like there are Elements in Nature, there are a few elements in Art also. These elements can be played with using principles (tools) of Composition. Whatever art form you may work with, this knowledge is a must. If not, your work looks like a work of craft rather than a work of art."

Dayakar lives in Hyderabad and is spending all his time with Reading, Writing and doing Paintings. He is not interested in mixing with people, likes only to live with his work other than his family and a few friends.

He says…" Even thousand years is not enough to master the art, so it is meaningless to waste my time with other things. I am not having that luxury. I am destined to understand Art."
He strongly believes what he says and has been living that way.

My website: http://maguntadayakar.com/

My Books on Art
How To Start A Painting And How To Plan It ?
How To Finish A Painting ?
Painting Landscapes From Imagination
Learn Composition and Create Beautiful Paintings
Simplified Color Schemes for Art Students
Capturing Movement in Portrait Painting
Who Fails As An Artist…? … One who loves his Paintings
Straight Talk On Painting and Painter's Problems
Abstract Realistic Painting Approach: Why it is the right approach for artists?
My Books on What is Painting and How to Learn it?
Character of the Creator: Do you have it in you?

My Paintings of Abstract Realism
How to Teach Sketching for Adults through 4 Simple Lessons and a few guidelines on painting

www.ingramcontent.com/pod-product-compliance
Lightning Source LLC
Chambersburg PA
CBHW070657220526
45466CB00001B/474